Teaching Little Fingers To Play American Tunes

Piano Solos with Optional Teacher Accompaniments

Arranged by
Eric Baumgartner

CONTENTS

Cover Design by Nick Gressle

ISBN 978-1-4234-6285-9

EXCLUSIVELY DISTRIBUTED BY

HAL•LEONARD®
7777 W. BLUEMOUND RD. P.O. BOX 13819
MILWAUKEE, WISCONSIN 53213

Visit Hal Leonard Online at
www.halleonard.com

Student Position
One Octave Higher When Performing as a Duet

This is, perhaps, the most famous American folksong. It was very popular even before the Revolutionary War. Folk songs are often created by singing new words over older, familiar melodies. For example, the words to "Yankee Doodle", written by an unknown English Army physician, are about our early American soldiers and are set to a melody that was already well known at that time in England and in America.

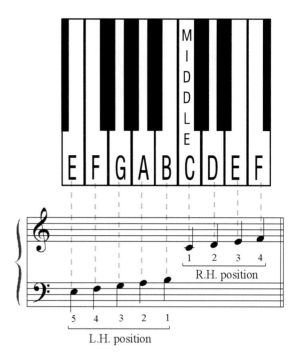

Yankee Doodle
Optional Teacher Accompaniment

arr. Eric Baumgartner

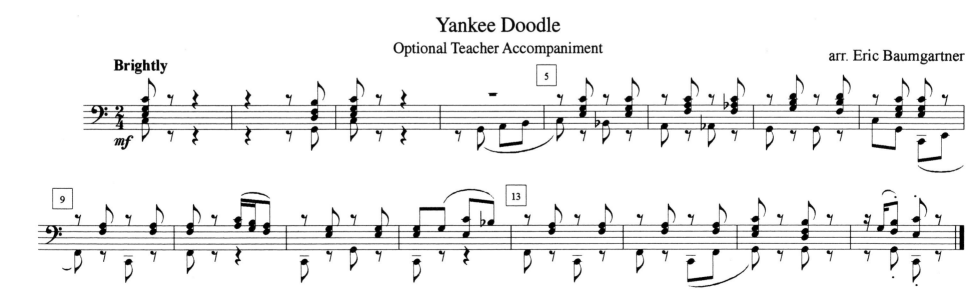

Yankee Doodle

Play both hands one octave higher when performing as a duet.

Traditional
arr. Eric Baumgartner

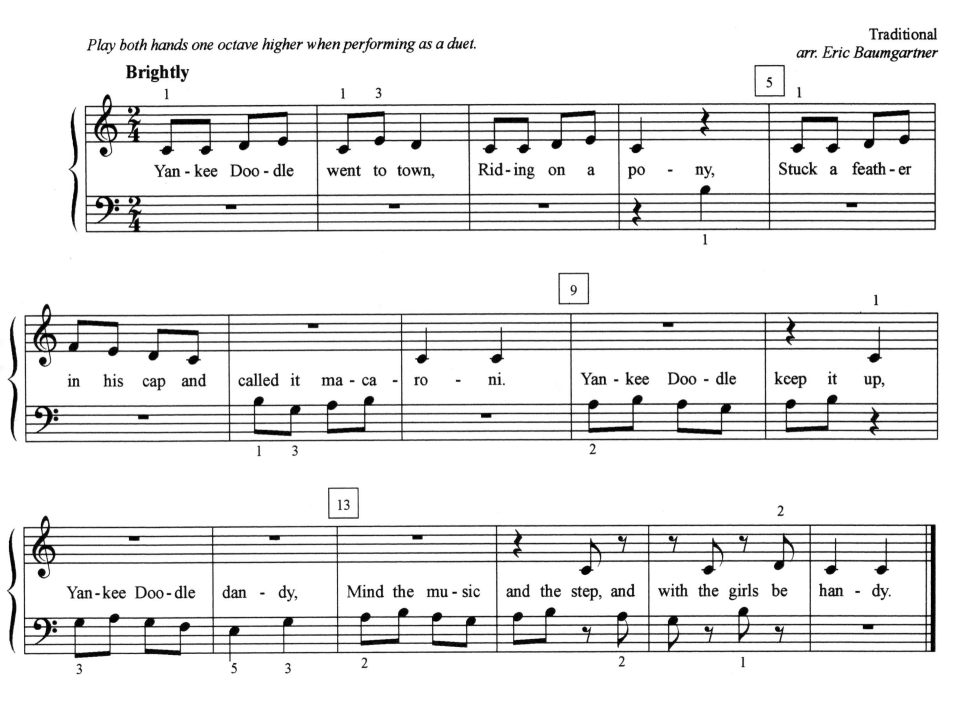

4

Student Position
One Octave Higher When Performing as a Duet

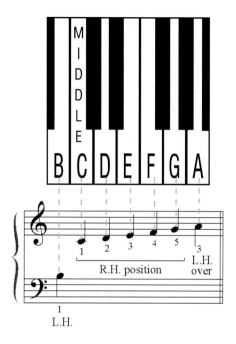

The words to "America" were written by the Reverend Samuel Francis Smith in 1831. The melody was borrowed from the English national anthem, "God Save the King (Queen)." It is not known who composed this tune. It has been very popular in Europe for centuries.

America
Optional Teacher Accompaniment

arr. Eric Baumgartner

America
(My Country 'Tis of Thee)

Samuel F. Smith

Traditional
arr. Eric Baumgartner

Play both hands one octave higher when performing as a duet.

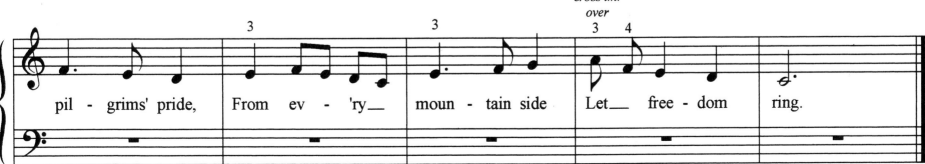

6

The words to this song were written during the Civil War by Patrick Gilmore, an Army musician. Gilmore borrowed the melody from an Irish folk song called "Johnny, I Hardly Knew Ye."

Student Position

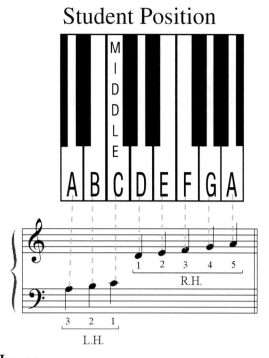

When Johnny Comes Marching Home

Optional Teacher Accompaniment

arr. Eric Baumgartner

Quickly

When Johnny Comes Marching Home

Patrick Gilmore

Traditional
arr. Eric Baumgartner

Student Position
One Octave Higher When Performing as a Duet

This is the Navy's song. It was first performed by the Navy Band during the 1906 Army-Navy football game. In fact, the first verse (which is included here) is basically a football fight song! The title, "Anchors Aweigh," means that the anchor has been raised from the bottom and that the ship is ready to sail.

Anchors Aweigh
Optional Teacher Accompaniment

arr. Eric Baumgartner

Anchors Aweigh

A. H. Miles and R. Lovell

Charles A. Zimmerman
arr. Eric Baumgartner

Play both hands one octave higher when performing as a duet.

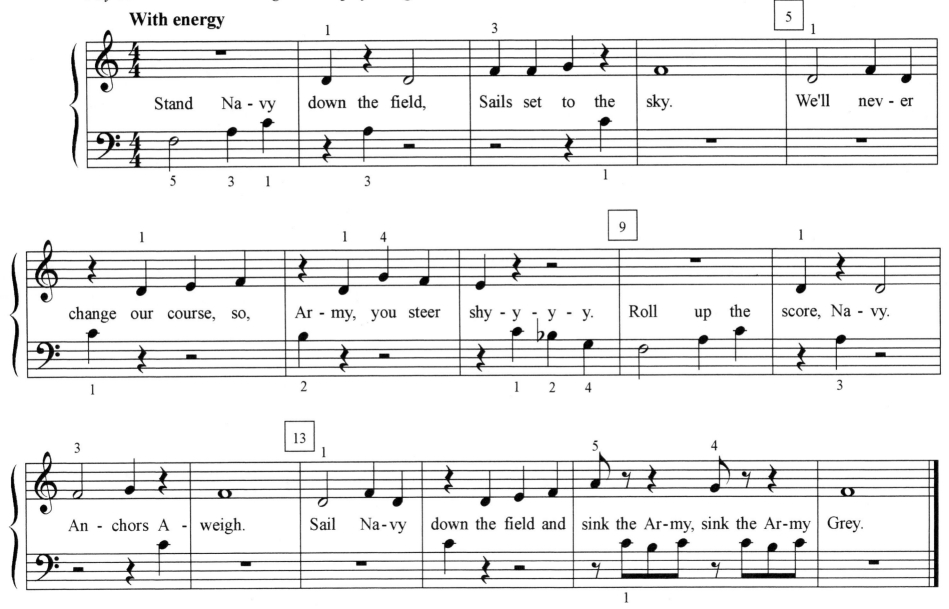

Student Position
One Octave Higher When Performing as a Duet

This song began as a poem written by Katherine Lee Bates in 1895. Many composers have set these moving words to music. This version, the best-known melody, was taken from a hymn composed by Samuel A. Ward.

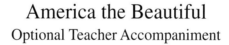

America the Beautiful
Optional Teacher Accompaniment

arr. Eric Baumgartner

America the Beautiful

Katherine Lee Bates

Samuel A. Ward
arr. Eric Baumgartner

Play both hands one octave higher when performing as a duet.

12

Student Position
One Octave Higher When Performing as a Duet

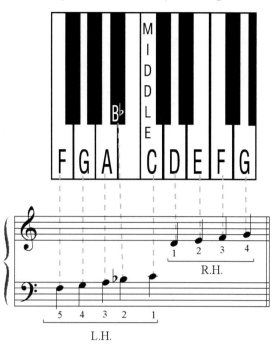

This song was written by Brigadier General Edmund L. Gruber when he was a first lieutenant stationed in the Philippines in 1908. Caissons were horse-drawn vehicles that carried ammunition. The words to this song were updated after World War II and it is now known as "The Army Song."

The Caissons Go Rolling Along
Optional Teacher Accompaniment

arr. Eric Baumgartner

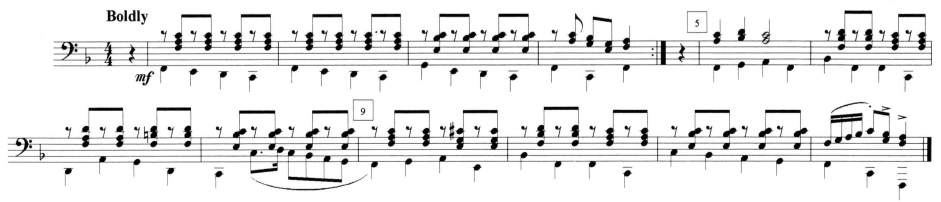

The Caissons Go Rolling Along

Play both hands one octave higher when performing as a duet.

Edmund L. Gruber
arr. Eric Baumgartner

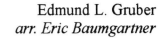

14

Student Position
One Octave Higher When Performing as a Duet

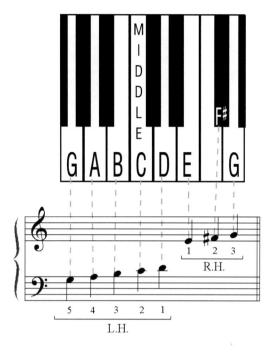

It is not exactly clear who wrote the words and music to the Marines' Hymn. An unknown Marine is said to have written the words in 1847. The music may have come from the French composer, Jacques Offenbach. Offenbach used this wonderful melody in his 1867 comic opera, *Geneviéve de Brabant.* Some believe, however, that the tune actually comes from a Spanish folk song, written well before Offenbach's opera.

The Marines' Hymn
Optional Teacher Accompaniment

arr. Eric Baumgartner

Vigorously

mf

The Marines' Hymn

Play both hands one octave higher when performing as a duet.

Music: Jacques Offenbach
arr. Eric Baumgartner

Student Position
One Octave Higher When Performing as a Duet

This song's melody was composed as a church hymn by William Steffe in the 1850's. The tune became so popular that many were writing new words to it during the Civil War. These, the most enduring lyrics, were written by Julia Ward Howe. She was inspired to write them after visiting some Army camps in 1861.

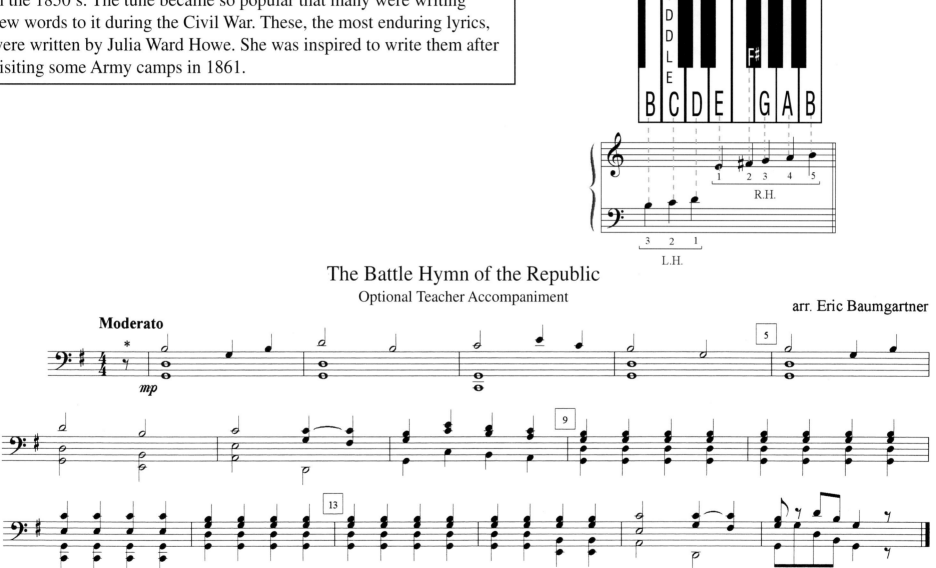

The Battle Hymn of the Republic
Optional Teacher Accompaniment

arr. Eric Baumgartner

Moderato

* *8th notes may be played in long-short pairs*

The Battle Hymn of the Republic

Julia Ward Howe

William Steffe
arr. Eric Baumgartner

Play both hands one octave higher when performing as a duet.

* 8th notes may be played in long-short pairs

Student Position
One Octave Higher When Performing as a Duet

"Dixie" was written in 1859 by Daniel Decatur Emmett. Emmett was a musician and a performer who wrote songs for traveling minstrel shows. Although the lyrics are about the good life in the South, the melody was quite a hit for both South and North during the Civil War.

Dixie
Optional Teacher Accompaniment

arr. Eric Baumgartner

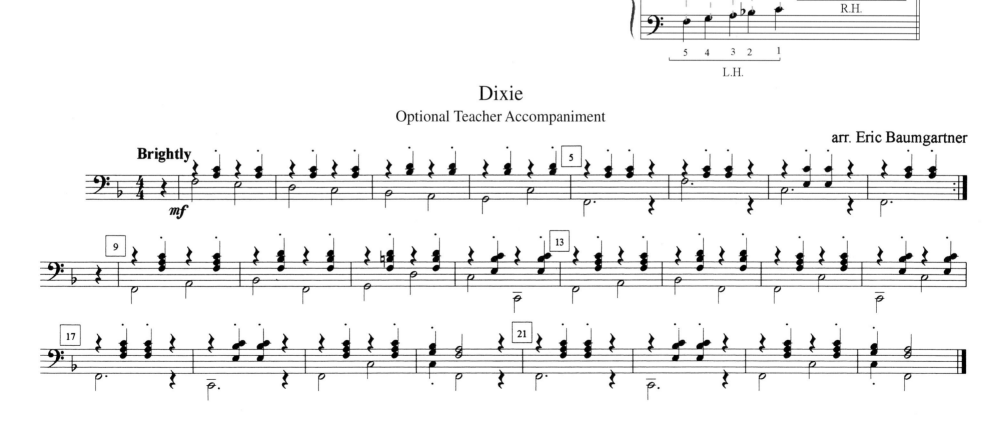

Dixie

Daniel Decatur Emmett
arr. Eric Baumgartner

Play both hands one octave higher when performing as a duet.

20

This is the best-loved song about America's pastime. Even though it was written in 1908, it is still sung at baseball games during the seventh inning stretch. Jack Norworth wrote the lyrics first and then approached Albert Von Tilzer to compose the music. Oddly enough, neither gentleman had ever attended a major league game before writing this baseball classic!

Take Me Out to the Ball Game

Optional Teacher Accompaniment

arr. Eric Baumgartner

Take Me Out to the Ball Game

Jack Norworth

Albert Von Tilzer
arr. Eric Baumgartner

Play both hands one octave higher when performing as a duet.

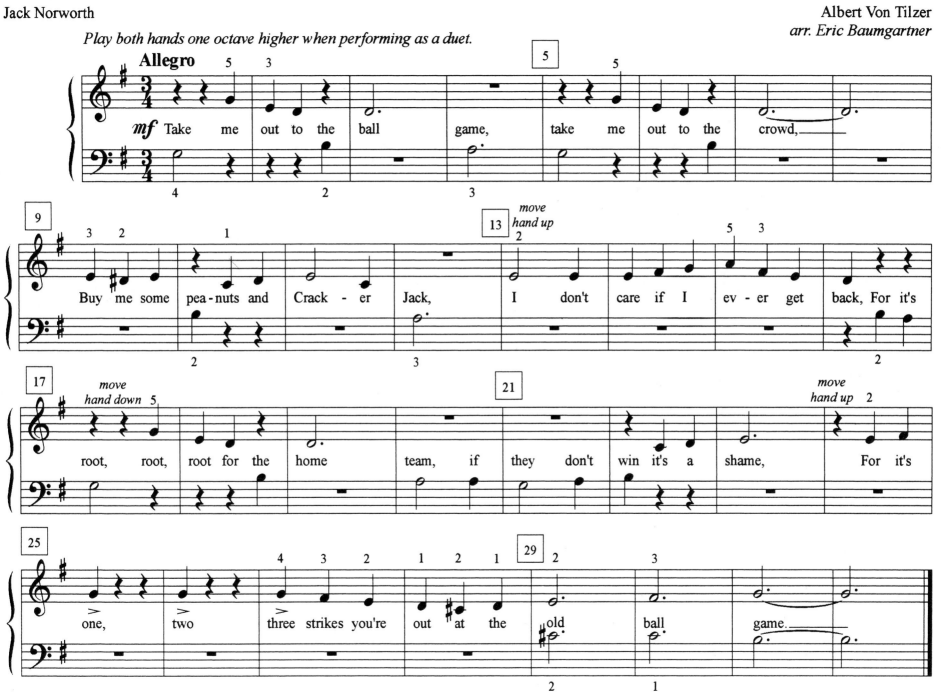

The words to our national anthem were written by Francis Scott Key in 1814. He wrote them after witnessing a battle between the U.S. and England at Fort McHenry during the War of 1812. The morning after the long battle he was relieved to see "that our flag was still there" flying over the fort. The melody was well known before Key wrote his poem: it is from an English song, "Anacreon in Heaven."

The Star-Spangled Banner
Optional Teacher Accompaniment

arr. Eric Baumgartner

The Star-Spangled Banner

Francis Scott Key

John Stafford Smith
arr. Eric Baumgartner

Play both hands one octave higher when performing as a duet.

This song was written in 1862 by George Frederick Root. Root wrote many popular songs for the North during the Civil War. This melody was so successful, however, that Southern soldiers sang it as well.

The Battle Cry of Freedom

George Frederick Root
arr. Eric Baumgartner

Play both hands one octave higher when performing as a duet.

Optional Teacher Accompaniment

arr. Eric Baumgartner